I0448131

September 2013

ICBM MODERNIZATION

Approaches to Basing Options and Interoperable Warhead Designs Need Better Planning and Synchronization

GAO-13-831

GAO Highlights

Highlights of GAO-13-831, a report to congressional committees

ICBM MODERNIZATION

Approaches to Basing Options and Interoperable Warhead Designs Need Better Planning and Synchronization

Why GAO Did This Study

U.S. nuclear weapons—both the bombs and warheads and their delivery systems—are aging beyond their intended service lives. The 2010 Nuclear Posture Review recommended that the Nuclear Weapons Council study options for extending the life of ICBM warheads, including the potential for developing a warhead that is interoperable on both Air Force and Navy missiles. In 2013 DOD will initiate a study to identify a replacement for the Minuteman III missile. This report addresses the extent to which (1) DOD has assessed the capability requirements, potential basing options, and costs for the follow-on to the Minuteman III ICBM; and (2) DOD and DOE have explored the feasibility of incorporating an interoperable warhead concept into the long-term nuclear weapons stockpile plan. GAO analyzed DOD and NNSA policies, plans, guidance, and other documents; and interviewed officials responsible for planning the Minuteman III follow-on and the warhead life-extension program.

What GAO Recommends

GAO is making seven recommendations to provide complete cost estimates to the Nuclear Weapons Council and improve synchronization between DOD and DOE; to identify long-term Navy funding to support the interoperable warhead life-extension program; and to issue or revise existing DOD and Nuclear Weapons Council guidance. In written comments on a draft of this report, DOD concurred with all of GAO's recommendations, and DOE concurred with the three recommendations requiring joint action between the two departments.

View GAO-13-831 or key components. For more information, contact John Pendleton at (202) 512-3489 or pendletonj@gao.gov.

What GAO Found

The Department of Defense (DOD) has identified capability requirements and potential basing options for the Minuteman III follow-on intercontinental ballistic missile (ICBM), and the Department of Energy (DOE) has begun a parallel study of options to extend the life of its warhead, but neither department plans to estimate the total system costs for the new missile and its warhead. GAO's work on cost estimating has found that a reliable cost estimate is critical to any program by providing the basis for informed decision making. The Nuclear Weapons Council—the joint activity of DOD and DOE for nuclear weapons programs—is responsible for coordinating budget matters related to nuclear weapons programs between the departments, and is engaging in an effort to broadly synchronize nuclear weapons life-extension programs with delivery-system modernization efforts, but has not asked either department to provide estimates of the total system cost. In the absence of such a request, neither department is developing total cost estimates. Further, DOD's plan to study ICBM follow-on options does not include the council as a stakeholder to synchronize the missile and warhead efforts to help ensure that the study considers an enterprise-wide perspective. Without timely cost estimates and updates on the status of the ICBM follow-on study, the council may be unable to provide guidance and direction on the study, or consider its implications and potential effects on other nuclear weapons modernization efforts.

DOD and DOE have prepared a long-term plan that incorporates interoperable warheads into the stockpile, and although they have begun studying the feasibility of designing such a warhead, the Navy has had limited participation thus far. The 2010 Nuclear Posture Review recommended the Nuclear Weapons Council study the development of an interoperable warhead that could be deployed on both Air Force and Navy ballistic missiles, and the council has requested the Air Force, Navy, and the National Nuclear Security Administration (NNSA) to commit resources to the study. Although the Air Force and NNSA have been examining warhead concepts, the Navy has not fully engaged in the effort because (1) other, ongoing modernization programs are higher Navy priorities, and (2) it has concerns about changing the design of the warhead. The Navy's further participation is uncertain because it has not identified the resources needed to continue with the program once the study is completed, if the interoperable warhead is adopted. Consequently, the Navy will be poorly positioned to perform the more-detailed analyses needed to validate the approved design, potentially resulting in program delays. The Nuclear Weapons Council guidelines governing nuclear weapons refurbishments, and the corresponding DOD instruction, do not require the Air Force and Navy to align their programs and resources before beginning joint-service warhead studies. For example, DOD's instruction states that the military departments are to develop procedures for certain joint DOD-DOE activities, but it is unclear about aligning their programs and resources with each other. If the guidance and DOD instruction are not updated, the services may not be prepared to participate in future joint-service studies.

_____ United States Government Accountability Office

Contents

Abbreviations

DOD	Department of Defense
DOE	Department of Energy
ICBM	intercontinental ballistic missile
New START	New Strategic Arms Reduction Treaty
NNSA	National Nuclear Security Administration
SLBM	submarine-launched ballistic missile

GAO U.S. GOVERNMENT ACCOUNTABILITY OFFICE

441 G St. N.W.
Washington, DC 20548

September 20, 2013

Congressional Committees

The 2010 *Nuclear Posture Review Report* affirmed that the fundamental role of U.S. nuclear weapons is to deter a nuclear attack against the United States, its allies, and partners.[1] U.S. strategic nuclear forces— intercontinental ballistic missiles (ICBM), submarine-launched ballistic missiles (SLBM), and nuclear-capable long-range bombers—continue to underwrite deterrence, albeit at substantially reduced levels from the Cold War. These delivery systems and the bombs and warheads they carry are aging, and some types of delivery systems are being deployed long beyond their intended service lives. For example, the Minuteman III ICBM was first deployed in 1970; following successive modernization efforts, it is expected to stay in service through 2030 as a highly responsive, alert nuclear force.[2] The current administration has pledged that the U.S. nuclear deterrent will be safe, secure, and effective for as long as nuclear weapons exist, even as it has committed to consider additional arms reductions. To this end, the Department of Defense (DOD) informed Congress in May 2012 that it intended to invest at least $118.5 billion to sustain and modernize nuclear delivery systems between fiscal year 2013 and fiscal year 2022,[3] while the National Nuclear Security Administration (NNSA), a separately organized agency within the Department of Energy (DOE), informed Congress in February 2011 that it had identified about

---

[1]Section 1070 of the National Defense Authorization Act for Fiscal Year 2008, Pub. L. No. 110-181 (2008), required the Secretary of Defense, in consultation with the Secretary of Energy and Secretary of State, to conduct a comprehensive review of the nuclear posture of the United States for the next 5 to 10 years. The Department of Defense (DOD) published the conclusions and recommendations from that review in the April 2010 *Nuclear Posture Review Report*.

[2]Section 139(a) of the John Warner National Defense Authorization Act for Fiscal Year 2007, Pub. L. No. 109-364 (2006), required the Air Force to modernize Minuteman III ICBMs in the inventory as required to maintain a sufficient supply of launch test assets and spares to sustain the deployed force of such missiles through 2030.

[3]Department of Defense, *Fiscal Year 2013 Report on the Plan for the Nuclear Weapons Stockpile, Nuclear Weapons Complex, Nuclear Weapons Delivery Systems, and Nuclear Weapons Command and Control System Specified in Section 1043 of the National Defense Authorization Act for Fiscal Year 2012* (Washington, D.C.: May 7, 2012).

$90 billion in nuclear weapons stockpile and infrastructure costs over roughly the same period.[4]

In 2013, the Air Force plans to initiate a study, called the Ground Based Strategic Deterrent analysis of alternatives (hereafter "Minuteman III follow-on study"), to identify the best approach to upgrade or replace the Minuteman III.[5] This study is being prepared under DOD's standard requirements and acquisition process, which generally begins when a military service or other sponsor identifies capability requirements and critical gaps, which may then be documented in an initial capabilities document.[6] The Joint Requirements Oversight Council approved the Air Force's initial capabilities document in August 2012, and since that time the Air Force has drafted a plan for conducting the Minuteman III follow-on study (hereafter "draft study plan"). As of April 2013, the Air Force expects that the study will begin later this fiscal year.

Even as the Air Force started planning for the Minuteman III follow-on study, in June 2012 the Nuclear Weapons Council requested that the Air Force, Navy, and NNSA study the feasibility and costs of options to extend the service life of the W78 ICBM warhead (hereafter "warhead feasibility study").[7] The council directed this study to recommend options for developing a warhead that not only would replace the W78 ICBM

---

[4]Department of Defense and Department of Energy, *Fiscal Year 2012 Annual Update to the Report Specified in Section 1251 of the National Defense Authorization Act for Fiscal Year 2010* (Washington, D.C.: Feb. 16, 2011).

[5]The Joint Requirements Oversight Council directed the Air Force to consider alternatives that replace, recapitalize, upgrade, or evolve existing ICBM capabilities. *See* Joint Requirements Oversight Council, JROCM 117-12, *Ground Based Strategic Deterrent Initial Capabilities Document* (Aug. 8, 2012).

[6]In DOD's requirements determination process, services, combatant commands, and other DOD components conduct capability-based assessments or other studies to assess capability requirements and associated gaps and risks. Any capability requirements that have significant gaps typically lead to an initial capabilities document, which can drive the development of solutions including new acquisitions. *See* Chairman of the Joint Chiefs of Staff Instruction 3170.01H, *Joint Capabilities Integration and Development System* (Jan. 10, 2012). An analysis of alternatives is generally conducted after a capability need is validated or approved through DOD's requirements determination process, and after a Materiel Development Decision is made.

[7]The Nuclear Weapons Council is a joint activity between DOD and DOE that is responsible for matters related to executive-level management of the nuclear weapons stockpile. *See* 10 U.S.C. § 179.

warhead,[8] but also could replace the W88 SLBM warhead. The resulting W78/88-1 warhead would be the first of three "interoperable warheads"—warheads designed with common (or "interoperable") nuclear explosive packages and similar (or "adaptable") nonnuclear components,[9] such that they are compatible with both Air Force and Navy ballistic missile systems—that the Nuclear Weapons Council envisions introducing to the stockpile over the next 25 years. This approach to warhead modernization marks a departure from prior ballistic missile warhead life-extension programs, which did not consider such options.

The W78/88-1 life-extension program is being conducted under the Nuclear Weapons Council's *Procedural Guideline for the Phase 6.X Process*,[10] which is used to manage nuclear weapons refurbishments, including not only alterations to replace aging nuclear weapons components, but also full-scope life-extension programs.[11] DOD procedures are further codified in a DOD instruction, *DOD Procedures for Joint DOD-DOE Nuclear Weapons Life-Cycle Activities*.[12] A joint DOD and DOE Project Officers Group provides day-to-day oversight and management of the warhead feasibility study.[13] The Air Force chairs the

---

[8]Technically, the design options to be considered would reuse existing nuclear components, some of which might require manufacturing, rather than "replace" the existing warheads with new types of nuclear weapons.

[9]Ballistic missile warheads consist of three sets of components—a primary, a secondary, and a set of nonnuclear components—all enclosed in a case, or aeroshell. When detonated, the primary and the secondary components, which together are referred to as the weapon's "nuclear explosive package," produce the weapon's explosive force, or "yield." The array of nonnuclear components controls and supports the detonation sequence and helps ensure the weapon's safety and security from human tampering and from environmental effects.

[10]Nuclear Weapons Council, *Procedural Guideline for the Phase 6.X Process* (Apr. 19, 2000).

[11]A full-scope life-extension program would refurbish an entire warhead at a system level, including nuclear and nonnuclear components, whereas a limited life-extension program would address one or several specific components or subassemblies.

[12]The instruction implements DOD guidance for defense acquisition as it applies to joint DOD-DOE nuclear weapon life-cycle activities, and the council's *Procedural Guideline for the Phase 6.X Process* as it applies to the refurbishment guidelines of the council. *See* Department of Defense Instruction 5030.55, *DOD Procedures for Joint DOD-DOE Nuclear Weapons Life-Cycle Activities* (Jan. 25, 2001).

[13]A "project officers group" coordinates the development and compatibility assurance of a designated nuclear weapon system and its associated interfaces.

Project Officers Group and the Navy serves as cochair. The Nuclear Weapons Council directed that the Project Officers Group complete the warhead feasibility study, identify potential costs for the warhead life-extension program, and recommend potential designs for council approval by December 31, 2014.

DOD and NNSA are beginning the effort to replace the Minuteman III and W78 warhead at a time of fiscal uncertainty. DOD plans to significantly reduce the rate of growth in defense spending over the next 5 years in response to the Budget Control Act of 2011 and the subsequent sequester. Since NNSA last reported its estimated nuclear weapons stockpile and infrastructure costs to Congress in February 2011, the agency had reprioritized nuclear modernization programs in response to fiscal uncertainties, including delaying key infrastructure projects and nuclear weapons life extensions. As the Minuteman III follow-on study and warhead feasibility study take shape, fiscal conditions affecting both DOD and DOE may create incentives for both departments to work more closely together to minimize risk, maximize value, and avoid a competition over scarce resources.

Section 1047 of the National Defense Authorization Act for Fiscal Year 2012 requires GAO to conduct a study of DOD's strategic nuclear weapons capabilities, force structure, employment policy, and targeting requirements.[14] This is the second unclassified report prepared in response to the requirement in the Act.[15] This report addresses the extent to which: (1) DOD has assessed the capability requirements, potential basing options, and costs for the follow-on to the Minuteman III ICBM; and (2) DOD and DOE have explored the feasibility of incorporating an

---

[14]Pub. L. No. 112-81, § 1047(a) (2011). Among other things, section 1047 requires GAO to cover in its study the following: an assessment of the requirements of DOD for strategic nuclear bomber aircraft and intercontinental ballistic missiles ("ICBM"), including assessments of the extent to which the Secretary of Defense has—(A) determined the force structure and capability requirements for nuclear-capable strategic bomber aircraft, bomber-delivered nuclear weapons, and ICBMs; (B) synchronized the requirements described in subparagraph (A) with plans to extend the service life of nuclear gravity bombs, nuclear-armed cruise missiles, and ICBM warheads; and (C) evaluated long-term ICBM alert posture requirements and basing options. *See* § 1047(b)(3). This report covers the matters related to ICBMs.

[15]Our first unclassified report covered the nuclear weapons targeting process. See GAO, *Strategic Weapons: Changes in the Nuclear Weapons Targeting Process Since 1991*, GAO-12-786R (Washington, D.C.: July 31, 2012).

interoperable warhead concept into the long-term nuclear weapons stockpile plan. In June 2013 we reported to you on the results of our work in a classified report. This is the unclassified version of that report. To prepare this unclassified version, we removed references to funding; stockpile quantities and locations; capabilities; and specific classified assessments.

To evaluate our objectives, we analyzed DOD, DOE, and Nuclear Weapons Council policies and guidance on the requirements development process and the planning and implementation of nuclear weapons delivery system modernization and stockpile life-extension programs. We obtained, reviewed, and analyzed key Air Force documents, such as the *Initial Capabilities Document for Ground Based Strategic Deterrent*,[16] and the Air Force's draft plan for preparing the Minuteman III follow-on study.[17] Using best practices we identified in our prior work,[18] we assessed the Air Force's proposed methodology for estimating the costs for options that the Air Force will consider in the Minuteman III follow-on study. We also reviewed DOD and NNSA reports, Project Officers Group and subgroup charters, and Air Force and NNSA budget documentation. We analyzed documents from the Office of the Secretary of Defense, Joint Staff, U.S. Strategic Command, NNSA, and the Nuclear Weapons Council. We also interviewed DOD and NNSA officials responsible for developing and coordinating requirements for the follow-on to the Minuteman III ICBM and for the W78/88-1 life-extension program, and other officials from the Office of the Secretary of Defense, including from the Office of the Deputy Assistant Secretary of Defense for Nuclear Matters and the Cost Assessment and Program Evaluation office; the Air Force, including Global Strike Command and Nuclear Weapons Center; the Navy, including Strategic Systems Programs; U.S. Strategic Command; and NNSA, including the manager for the W78/88-1 life-extension program and managers for the ICBM and SLBM weapons systems.

---

[16]Air Force Global Strike Command, *Initial Capabilities Document for Ground Based Strategic Deterrent*, version 1.06 (June 4, 2012).

[17]Air Force Global Strike Command, Draft *Ground Based Strategic Deterrent Analysis of Alternatives Study Plan* (Nov. 20, 2012).

[18]GAO, *GAO Cost Estimating and Assessment Guide: Best Practices for Developing and Managing Capital Program Costs*, GAO-09-3SP (Washington, D.C.: March 2009).

We conducted this performance audit from June 2012 to June 2013 in accordance with generally accepted government auditing standards. Those standards require that we plan and perform the audit to obtain sufficient, appropriate evidence to provide a reasonable basis for our findings and conclusions based on our audit objectives. We believe that the evidence obtained provides a reasonable basis for our findings and conclusions based on our audit objectives. Our scope and methodology are described in more detail in appendix I.

Background

The Air Force presently deploys 450 Minuteman III ICBMs in fixed, land-based launch facilities (or "silos"), located on three bases that encompass vast regions of the United States. Three missile wings—the 90th Missile Wing, 91st Missile Wing, and 341st Missile Wing, which fall under the command of Air Force Global Strike Command—operate the ICBM force. Each ICBM carries up to three W78 warheads, or a single W87 warhead. In fiscal year 2007, the Air Force began deploying W87 warheads, while reducing the number of deployed W78 warheads. To support U.S. Strategic Command's operational requirements, the Air Force maintains nearly all of the ICBMs on alert at any given time.[19]

DOD has not finalized the force structure and warhead requirements for the Minuteman III under the New Strategic Arms Reduction Treaty (New START).[20] DOD last reported on its plans to implement the treaty in May 2012, when it informed Congress that the Air Force would deploy up to 420 Minuteman III ICBMs by 2018,[21] each carrying only a single warhead. Based on the 2010 *Nuclear Posture Review Report*, the Air Force plans to retain the ability to redeploy additional warheads on the Minuteman III in case technical problems occur with other strategic delivery systems or warheads. In April 2013, DOD informed Congress that the decision on how to meet the New START limits will be finalized before the beginning of fiscal year 2015.

---

[19]The 2010 Nuclear Posture Review concluded that the United States should maintain the current posture of nearly all ICBMs on alert.

[20]*Treaty on Measures for the Further Reduction and Limitation of Strategic Offensive Arms*, U.S.-Russ., Apr. 8, 2010, S. Treaty Doc. No. 111-5 (2010).

[21]DOD also reported the intent to maintain up to 454 deployed and nondeployed ICBM launchers, which include several test assets, in order to comply with New START.

Like the Air Force, the Navy also maintains and operates nuclear-armed ballistic missiles. Nuclear-armed Trident II SLBMs are deployed on 14 Ohio-class fleet ballistic missile submarines, 12 of which are operational at any given time, while 2 are in overhaul. Each submarine currently carries 24 SLBMs, and each SLBM carries either multiple W76-0/1 warheads or W88 warheads.[22] NNSA is refurbishing the W76 warhead, and plans to upgrade key nonnuclear components of the W88 warhead beginning in fiscal year 2019. Unlike the Air Force, not all of the Navy's ballistic missile force structure is on alert at any given time.

Since 1994, the United States has retained a stockpile of nondeployed weapons, called the hedge, in order to mitigate risks posed by unforeseen technical problems with deployed weapons, or posed by changes in the international security environment. As of September 2012, the Air Force maintained both W78 warheads and W87 warheads in the hedge, and the Navy maintained W76-0/1 warheads in the hedge. All of the Navy's W88 warheads are either operationally deployed or retained as spares to be used when deployed weapons are withdrawn for maintenance.

Air Force and Navy warheads were designed with unique aeroshells, which differ in size, weight, and payload capacities. The W78 warhead is encased in the Air Force Mk12A aeroshell, and the W87 warhead is encased in the Mk21 aeroshell. The W88 warhead is encased in the Navy's Mk5 aeroshell, which, while smaller than the Mk21, is comparable to the Mk21 in volume and payload capacity.

A number of DOD and DOE organizations oversee the nuclear weapons enterprise, which includes the military forces, military and civilian organizations, nuclear weapons design laboratories, and nuclear weapons production plants that support DOD's nuclear deterrence mission:

- DOD and DOE, specifically NNSA, share responsibility under the Phase 6.X process for nuclear weapons refurbishments and life-extension programs. In addition to the W78/88-1 life-extension program, NNSA is producing W76-1 warheads for the Navy, and plans to begin producing B61-12 gravity bombs for the Air Force in

---

[22]NNSA is in the process of extending the service life of the W76-0 warhead. The refurbished warhead is referred to as the W76-1.

fiscal year 2019. NNSA also plans to initiate a life-extension program for a cruise missile warhead, with production beginning in 2024.

- The Air Force and Navy develop strategic delivery systems such as ICBMs and SLBMs, and provide personnel, training, and equipment for nuclear operations. In addition to the effort to replace the Minuteman III ICBM, the Air Force plans to replace the nuclear-armed air-launched cruise missile and develop a new, nuclear-capable bomber. The Navy is acquiring a replacement for the Ohio-class submarine, and plans to replace the Trident II SLBM in the 2040s.

- Air Force Global Strike Command provides operational ICBM forces and is responsible for preparing the Minuteman III follow-on study, and the Air Force Nuclear Weapons Center oversees Minuteman III sustainment activities. The Air Force Nuclear Weapons Center also chairs the W78/88-1 Project Officers Group.

- Navy Strategic Systems Programs is the Navy's technical authority for nuclear weapons systems and strategic forces; engages in activities for Navy SLBMs and warhead requirements and modernization; and chairs the project officers groups for Navy warheads. Strategic Systems Programs cochairs the W78/88-1 Project Officers Group with the Air Force.

- The Commander of U.S. Strategic Command, following guidance and direction provided by the President, Secretary of Defense, and Chairman of the Joint Chiefs of Staff, develops an operational plan and identifies targets for nuclear forces.

- NNSA's Office of Defense Programs plans and coordinates NNSA activities to maintain the nuclear weapons stockpile. A national complex of three nuclear weapons design laboratories, four production plants, and the Nevada National Security Site carry out the Office of Defense Programs' mission. NNSA plans to modernize its plutonium and uranium processing capabilities at Los Alamos, New Mexico, and Oak Ridge, Tennessee, respectively. Lawrence Livermore National Laboratory, in California, Los Alamos National Laboratory, in New Mexico, and Sandia National Laboratories, in New Mexico and California, are involved in the warhead feasibility study.

The Nuclear Weapons Council is the joint DOD and DOE activity responsible for matters related to executive-level management of the nuclear weapons stockpile.[23] Established by statute in 1986,[24] the council facilitates cooperation and coordination between the two departments to evaluate, maintain, and ensure the safety, security, and control of the nuclear weapons stockpile. Among its responsibilities, the Nuclear Weapons Council prepares the Nuclear Weapons Stockpile Memorandum on behalf of the Secretaries of Defense and Energy,[25] which is transmitted to the President and, if approved, serves as the basis for the Nuclear Weapons Stockpile Plan. In November 2012, to synchronize NNSA nuclear weapons life-extension programs, DOD platform modernization programs, and NNSA plans for recapitalizing key nuclear weapons production infrastructure, the Nuclear Weapons Council adopted a long-term baseline plan for the nuclear weapons enterprise.[26] The council's baseline plan featured the development of interoperable warheads, beginning with the W78/88-1 life-extension program.

[23]The Nuclear Weapons Council is chaired by the Under Secretary of Defense for Acquisition, Technology and Logistics, and its members include the Under Secretary of Defense for Policy, the Vice Chairman of the Joint Chiefs of Staff, the Commander of U.S. Strategic Command, and the Under Secretary of Energy for Nuclear Security (who also serves as the Administrator of NNSA).The Under Secretary of Energy for Nuclear Security serves as the chair at meetings where a matter under consideration is within the primary responsibility or concern of DOE as determined by council vote. *See* 10 U.S.C. § 179.

[24]*See* National Defense Authorization Act for Fiscal Year 1987, Pub. L. No. 99-661, § 3137(a) (1986) (codified as amended at 10 U.S.C. § 179).

[25]*See* 10 U.S.C. § 179(d)(1). The Secretaries of Defense and Energy last submitted a Nuclear Weapons Stockpile Memorandum to the President in February 2011. The current plan is published as Presidential Policy Directive 9, *Fiscal Years 2011–2017 Nuclear Weapons Stockpile Plan.*

[26]Nuclear Weapons Council, *Joint Department of Energy/National Nuclear Security Administration and Department of Defense Programmatic Decisions, Attachment 1, Nuclear Weapons Council Baseline Plan*, Memorandum for Members of the Nuclear Weapons Council (Jan. 15, 2013).

DOD Has Identified Potential Minuteman III Follow-on Options but DOD and NNSA Are Not Preparing Complete Cost Estimates or Effectively Involving the Nuclear Weapons Council

DOD has identified capability requirements and potential basing options for the Minuteman III follow-on ICBM; however, neither the Air Force nor NNSA are required to estimate the total system costs for both the missile and warhead for the Nuclear Weapons Council to review; moreover, the Air Force does not identify the council as a stakeholder to synchronize the Minuteman III follow-on study with the W78/88-1 life-extension program. The potential options under consideration in the Minuteman III follow-on study include maintaining the existing Minuteman III, upgrading the Minuteman III, and developing a new missile on mobile launchers. Although the Nuclear Weapons Council is responsible for coordinating budget matters pertaining to nuclear weapons programs between DOD and DOE, and is engaging in an effort to broadly synchronize warhead life-extension programs with delivery system modernization efforts, it has not requested that either the Air Force or NNSA estimate the total system costs of the missile and warhead. Moreover, neither the Air Force nor NNSA are required to prepare cost estimates that identify the total system costs for both the Minuteman III follow-on system and the W78/88-1 warhead for the Nuclear Weapons Council's review. Furthermore, the Air Force has not identified the council as a stakeholder to provide guidance on synchronizing the Minuteman III follow-on study with the W78/88-1 life-extension program, even though it is responsible for coordinating the programming of nuclear weapons programs between DOD and NNSA, such as a nuclear weapon life-extension program. Without timely and relevant information on the projected costs and findings of the Minuteman III follow-on study, the Nuclear Weapons Council may be unable to provide guidance to the Air Force on the study, or consider the study's implications and potential effects on other nuclear weapons modernization efforts as it revises its baseline plan.

DOD Has Identified Capability Requirements and Alternative Basing Options to Be Analyzed in the Minuteman III Follow-on Study

DOD has identified capability requirements and alternative basing options to be analyzed in the Minuteman III follow-on study, consistent with the 2010 *Nuclear Posture Review Report*. With this review, DOD was directed to study potential alternatives for the Minuteman III, with the objective of defining a cost-effective approach that supports continued reductions in U.S. nuclear weapons while maintaining stable deterrence. To prepare the initial capabilities document, the Air Force examined a range of potential scenarios involving nuclear combat between 2025 and 2075, and concluded that ICBMs provide a stabilizing influence through dispersed basing, alert posture, and high day-to-day readiness. However, the initial capabilities document also found that while the Minuteman III currently provides a robust deterrent, it is an aging weapon system that requires enhancement, recapitalization, replacement, or development of a new capability. The Air Force's list of ICBM capability requirements is presented in table 1.

Table 1: ICBM Capability Requirements

Capability	Description
Adaptable	Includes modular and common technologies that will reduce ownership costs and improve sustainability over the long term
Effective	Delivers the required probability of damage to meet the commander's intent, given anticipated weapon yields
Flexible	Delivers relatively comparable effects that are proportional to an adversary's actions and achieves the commander's intent across a range of different scenarios
Global	Conducts worldwide operations with the ability to reach assigned targets, particularly those that are high value
Reliable	System promotes high confidence that a strike, once ordered, will be consistently executed and continues to perform at current reliability levels or better
Responsive	Operates within specified time constraints; high availability with connectivity to a secure, redundant, and immediate command and control capability
Safe	Includes design features to maintain the weapon in a safe configuration, and minimize the possibility of nuclear detonation due to accidents, inadvertent errors, or acts of nature
Secure	Measures to deny unauthorized access to the nuclear weapon, supporting systems, and critical components
Survivable	Sufficiently dispersed and/or hardened to achieve survivability against a direct attack and capable of executing in pre-, trans-, and postattack scenarios
Sustainable	Provides affordable, maintainable, feasible, and executable systems across operational lifetime and sustained performance while maintaining low total life-cycle costs
Transportable	Possesses compatibility with mobility aircraft, ground transportation, and handling equipment, and can be safely loaded and unloaded in safe, secure environments

Source: Air Force Global Strike Command, (data); GAO (presentation).

Note: Capability requirements are identified in Air Force Global Strke Command, *Initial Capabilities Document for Ground Based Strategic Deterrent,* v 1.06 (June 4, 2012).

The Air Force plans to formally assess different alternatives to replace, recapitalize, upgrade, or evolve the existing Minuteman III ICBM during the follow-on study. In preparation for the study, the Air Force has developed a list of potential basing options, which it used to categorize the alternatives to be assessed in the follow-on study. As of March 2013, according to the Air Force Global Strike Command and Air Force Nuclear Weapons Center, the Air Force has identified five potential approaches for replacing the Minuteman III, as summarized in table 2. However, Air Force officials added that these basing options could change before the Minuteman III follow-on study begins later this year.

Table 2: ICBM Basing Options to Be Considered in the Minuteman III Follow-on Study, as of March 2013

Name	Description
Baseline	Maintain the Minuteman III ICBM and supporting infrastructure through limited refurbishments and replacements of existing parts.
Current Fixed	Upgrade the Minuteman III over time with more-effective modular components, such as a new guidance system, to meet emerging threats while maintaining the existing silo infrastructure.
New Fixed	Build a new ICBM with enhanced capabilities in new superhardened, fixed silos to enhance the system's survivability against a potential attack.
Mobile	Build a new ICBM with enhanced components that would be placed on a mobile transport system that would be stored in garrison shelters, and would be capable of dispersing to launch points during alert periods.
Tunnel	Build a new ICBM with enhanced components that would be based in a hardened underground tunnel with multiple launch points, along a 10 to 20 mile track, and a system to periodically transport the missile to these launch points to increase positional uncertainty and enhance survivability.

Source: Air Force Nuclear Weapons Center (data); GAO (presentation).

The Air Force recognizes that there are benefits and risks for each of the basing options. For example, the New Fixed, Mobile, and Tunnel approaches might enhance the system's survivability, according to Air Force Nuclear Weapons Center documentation and officials from the Office of the Secretary of Defense. However, the Air Force recognizes that there are risks to each approach, noting for example that introducing new technologies to legacy systems could create technical risk for either the Baseline or Current Fixed approaches.

Air Force officials expect that there will be a wide range of costs associated with each basing option. Air Force officials noted that they do not plan on ruling out options prior to the start of the Minuteman III follow-on study because of cost, but added that cost will likely play a considerable role during the study. For example, in 2005 during the Land Based Strategic Deterrent analysis of alternatives,[27] the Air Force reviewed several basing options including mobile and rail variants. During that study, officials requested the Air Force to narrow its scope to finish the study more quickly, according to U.S. Strategic Command and Air Force Global Strike Command officials. The Air Force official added that the mobile and rail variants were quickly eliminated based on their

---

[27]The 2003 *Nuclear Posture Review Implementation Plan* directed the Air Force to conduct an analysis of alternatives for a follow-on ICBM capability to be operational by 2018. The Air Force completed the Land Based Strategic Deterrent analysis of alternatives in 2005, but the program never moved to the next stage of the acquisition process, according to Air Force officials.

estimated costs in order to meet this direction. As of March 2013, the Air Force plans on assessing mobile and underground rail options during the current study with a different set of assumptions than were used in the previous study, primarily the ability of options to maintain a resilient deterrent effect at lower force levels, according to Air Force Global Strike Command. Final direction on study options will occur when the analysis formally begins.

The Air Force and NNSA Are Not Developing Complete System Cost Estimates for the Nuclear Weapons Council

The Nuclear Weapons Council is synchronizing DOD programs to modernize delivery systems with NNSA warhead life-extension programs, but neither the Air Force nor NNSA are preparing cost estimates that identify the total system costs for both the Minuteman III follow-on system and the W78/88-1 warhead. GAO's work on cost estimating has found that a reliable cost estimate is critical to the success of any program because it provides the basis for informed decision making. Furthermore, it is important to provide such information early to effectively inform decision making in the acquisition process. The Nuclear Weapons Council needs such information to effectively synchronize DOD and NNSA budgeting plans for nuclear weapons modernization.

Although the Nuclear Weapons Council should have estimates for the full system cost for the Minuteman III follow-on system, neither the Air Force nor NNSA are estimating such costs. Our review of the Air Force's draft plan for estimating Minuteman III follow-on costs indicates that, if the plan is followed, the cost estimates will likely be well documented, accurate, and credible in terms of estimating costs for the missile system itself. However, from a system-wide perspective, the Air Force's draft methodology is not comprehensive, because the Air Force is not including the costs for the W78/88-1 warhead in its estimate. DOD officials told us that the Air Force is not responsible for estimating the costs for the W78/88-1 life-extension program as it prepares the Minuteman III follow-on study. According to senior officials from the Office of the Secretary of Defense, Air Force, and NNSA, NNSA is responsible for planning, programming, and budgeting for the costs for the W78/88-1 warhead, regardless of whether or how the Air Force replaces the Minuteman III ICBM.

Further, NNSA believes it is premature to prepare cost estimates for the W78/88-1 warhead life extension because, according to NNSA officials, doing so requires making assumptions about the warhead's design and mode of deployment. The federal program manager and other NNSA officials stated that reliable estimates for the warhead's development and production costs could not be prepared until additional information was known about the specific nuclear explosive package design, enhanced safety features, and the Air Force's basing of the Minuteman III follow-on system. NNSA officials told us that preliminary cost estimates for the W78/88-1 life-extension program, prepared in October 2012, for the *Fiscal Year 2014 Stockpile Stewardship Management Plan*, total about $12 billion in fiscal year 2012 dollars, but they noted that this estimate is uncertain and likely to change as both the Minuteman III follow-on study and the warhead feasibility study make progress over the next 2 years. NNSA officials expect to prepare long-term cost estimates for this and other warhead life-extension programs as NNSA develops its agency-wide stockpile management plan, but these estimates do not include cost estimates for DOD's delivery system modernization efforts, and are not being prepared in conjunction with the Minuteman III follow-on study. The Nuclear Weapons Council directed the Project Officers Group—the group that exercises day-to-day management of the warhead feasibility study— to provide it with a semiannual program review on the study, and stated that nuclear enterprise life-cycle costs will be a key metric in selecting a design for the warhead. However, the Project Officers Group is not required to provide a final cost estimate to the council until December 2014.

Given the lack of synchronization between DOD's and DOE's cost estimate preparation, it is critical that the Nuclear Weapons Council understand the full potential system costs for replacing the Minuteman III and developing the W78/88-1 warhead. Without this understanding, the council will not have the key information it needs to synchronize planning and programming of nuclear weapons activities across DOD and DOE. Moreover, it is not clear which department will bear responsibility for the total system costs. For example, in 2010 DOD transferred $5.7 billion of budget authority to NNSA for nuclear weapons and naval reactor program activities from 2011 to 2015, including $784 million for the warhead life-extension program. DOD later augmented this $5.7 billion with an additional $2.2 billion to be allocated annually from fiscal year 2012 to fiscal year 2016. However, neither the Air Force nor NNSA are preparing total system costs estimates for the missile and warhead, or formally providing such estimates to the council.

The Air Force's Draft Plan Does Not Effectively Involve the Nuclear Weapons Council

The Nuclear Weapons Council is responsible for coordinating programming and budget matters pertaining to nuclear weapons programs between DOD and DOE, but the Air Force's draft plan does not identify the council as a formal stakeholder to synchronize the two studies. According to Air Force and NNSA officials, they are establishing procedures to synchronize the Minuteman III follow-on study with NNSA's warhead feasibility study. Air Force officials noted that the Minuteman III follow-on study group is working with the W78/88-1 Project Officers Group to identify potential integration challenges. NNSA officials told us that the group will help both the Air Force and NNSA to anticipate key requirements for designing the communications interface between the new missile and its warhead. Air Force and NNSA officials added that these integration challenges are expected to be addressed in the future.

Although the Air Force and NNSA are establishing relationships to ensure requirements are synchronized, the Air Force has not identified the Nuclear Weapons Council as a stakeholder in the Minuteman III follow-on study. An Air Force handbook on performing operations analysis indicates that organizations that are heavily invested in the outcome of an analysis should be given consideration as stakeholders.[28] According to a senior official in the Office of the Secretary of Defense, the Minuteman III follow-on study's ongoing status, potential recommendations, cost estimates, and program schedule for the new missile are important factors for the Nuclear Weapons Council to consider as it synchronizes the nuclear modernization efforts across DOD and DOE.

Rather than identifying the Nuclear Weapons Council as a key stakeholder, the Air Force's November 2012 draft plan designates senior DOD and NNSA representatives as members of a specially created study advisory group, which is the only body authorized to change the study guidance, and thus the scope and direction of the Air Force's analysis. Each of the Nuclear Weapons Council's member offices is to be represented on the study advisory group and will receive periodic updates on the Minuteman III follow-on study's progress and findings, according to the Air Force's draft study plan. Some Air Force and U.S. Strategic Command officials told us that this process may be sufficient to obtain the council's perspective.

---

[28]Air Force Materiel Command, Office of Aerospace Studies, *Air Force Analyst's Handbook: On Understanding the Nature of Analysis* (Kirtland Air Force Base, N.M.: January 2000).

In contrast, several other officials from across DOD and DOE stated that the Nuclear Weapons Council should be formally identified as a key stakeholder in the draft study plan to help ensure that the Air Force considers an enterprise-wide perspective as it conducts the study. For example, officials from the Office of the Secretary of Defense and some Air Force officials stated that the study advisory group members may not approach their responsibilities from an operational or DOD-wide policy perspective. Additionally, a senior official from the Office of the Secretary of Defense highlighted the need for the Nuclear Weapons Council to be cognizant of how NNSA's life-extension program activities support the Air Force's schedule for developing and fielding the Minuteman III follow-on system. Air Force Global Strike Command and other Office of the Secretary of Defense officials told us that it would be beneficial for the Nuclear Weapons Council to review the conduct and findings of the Minuteman III follow-on study to ensure the program is managed from an enterprise-wide perspective. NNSA officials added that including the Nuclear Weapons Council as a stakeholder would improve NNSA's understanding of the Air Force's priorities for the Minuteman III follow-on system relative to other Air Force modernization priorities. A senior official from the Air Force Nuclear Weapons Center stated that including the Nuclear Weapons Council as a stakeholder could bring focus and high-level attention to the council's planning effort.

Without timely and relevant information on the progress and findings of the Minuteman III follow-on study, the Nuclear Weapons Council may not be able to provide guidance on synchronizing the Minuteman III follow-on program with the W78/88-1 life-extension program, or consider the study's implications and potential effects on other nuclear weapons modernization efforts. The Nuclear Weapons Council expects to update and revise its baseline plan for the nuclear weapons enterprise in 2013 based on information obtained from ongoing weapons modernization programs and analyses. Such revisions could include adjusting the schedule of key weapons modernization programs, including the W78/88-1 life-extension program. In preparing the long-term baseline plan that it adopted in November 2012, the Nuclear Weapons Council recommended adjusting initial operational dates for multiple nuclear weapons systems and warhead life-extension programs. Absent accurate and reliable information on nuclear weapons programs such as the Minuteman III follow-on program, the Nuclear Weapons Council may be poorly positioned to consider such changes in the future.

DOD and DOE's Long-Term Plan for the Nuclear Weapons Enterprise Incorporates Interoperable Warheads, but the Navy's Participation in the Warhead Feasibility Study Has Been Limited

DOD and DOE, through the Nuclear Weapons Council, have prepared a long-term, baseline plan for the nuclear weapons enterprise that incorporates interoperable warheads, and the Air Force and NNSA have begun examining the feasibility of designing such a warhead, but the modernization of existing weapons is a higher Navy priority and has limited the Navy's participation in the warhead feasibility study.[29] The 2010 Nuclear Posture Review recommended that the Nuclear Weapons Council study options for extending the life of the W78 ICBM warhead, including the possibility of using the resulting warhead also on Navy SLBMs, and in June 2012 the Nuclear Weapons Council requested the Air Force, Navy, and NNSA to commit resources to the W78/88-1 life-extension program study. Although the Air Force and NNSA have been examining interoperable warhead concepts at the council's direction, the Navy had not included funds in its fiscal year 2013 budget submission for the effort because the ongoing W76-1 life-extension program and other modernization efforts were higher priorities, and because the Navy had concerns about introducing changes to the design of Navy warheads. The Navy's fiscal year 2014 budget submission did include funds for the study; however, according to the Air Force, the Navy's limited participation to date has delayed the Project Officer Group's review of key requirements. Moreover, unless the Navy identifies the resources needed to implement the later stages of the life-extension program, should the Nuclear Weapons Council approve the W78/88-1 interoperable design, the Navy may not be in a position to test and certify the resulting design or take other steps needed to prepare it for deployment. Lastly, if the guidance governing life-extension programs is not updated, the services may not be prepared to align their programs and resources in support of joint interoperable warhead studies.

---

[29]The National Defense Authorization Act for Fiscal Year 2013 included a provision requiring the Secretary of the Navy and the Secretary of the Air Force to submit separate statements to the Nuclear Weapons Council on plans related to a combined or interoperable warhead, and views of each secretary. The council is to submit a report to congressional defense committees related to the combined or interoperable warhead and include the views of the council and the statements of the secretaries. *See* Pub. L. No. 112-239, § 1044 (2013).

The Nuclear Weapons Council's Baseline Plan for the Nuclear Weapons Enterprise Incorporates Interoperable Warheads

The Nuclear Weapons Council's baseline plan for the nuclear weapons enterprise, adopted in November 2012, establishes a long-term vision for the stockpile that is built around the development of interoperable ballistic missile warheads. The first interoperable warhead, as shown in figure 1, would be produced beginning with the W78/88-1 life-extension program in 2025; a second interoperable ballistic missile warhead would be produced beginning in 2031; and a third type beginning in 2037, according to the Nuclear Weapons Council's baseline plan.

Figure 1: First Production Unit Dates for Interoperable Ballistic Missile Warheads as of November 2012

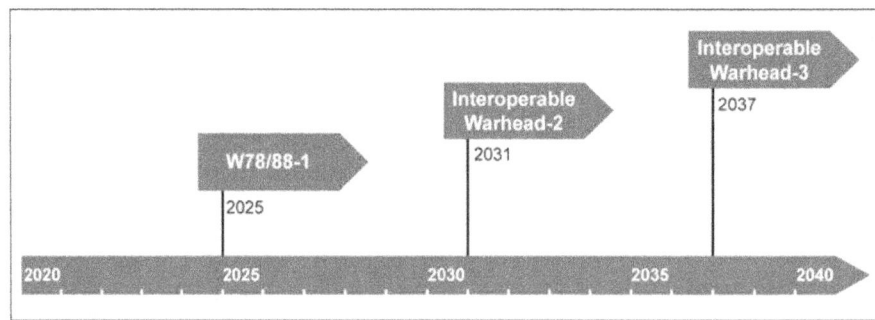

Source: Nuclear Weapons Council (data); GAO (presentation).

Note: As of March 2013, Navy and NNSA officials were uncertain whether the plan envisions the Navy withdrawing the W88 warhead from the stockpile and replacing it with the W78/88-1, or keeping the W88 in the stockpile until the second interoperable warhead is produced.

A key reason for developing the interoperable W78/88-1 warhead is that it would provide U.S. Strategic Command flexibility to adjust its nuclear war plan, should deployed warheads develop safety, security, or effectiveness problems due to age or unforeseen technical failure, according to DOD and NNSA. For example, as of September 30, 2012, SLBM W76-0/1 warheads accounted for a significant percentage of the deployed U.S. nuclear force. Should these weapons become unreliable, the Navy would not have replacements available because all of the W88 warheads in the stockpile are already factored into the nuclear war plan. Rather, DOD would have to deploy additional ICBM warheads and weapons carried by heavy bombers, which could create operational risks because ICBM warheads and bomber weapons have different operational characteristics—such as range, accuracy, yield, fuzing options, and responsiveness—than do SLBM warheads.[30] By adding interoperable warheads to the stockpile, DOD would have additional flexibility to ensure target coverage in the war plan if the W76-0/1 warheads were unexpectedly withdrawn from operations, because the Navy would have another type of SLBM warhead available to replace it.

The Air Force and NNSA Have Begun Examining the Feasibility of the W78/88-1 Warhead with Limited Navy Participation

Even before the Nuclear Weapons Council adopted its nuclear weapons enterprise baseline plan, the Air Force and NNSA completed a concept study and initiated a feasibility study for the W78/88-1 life-extension program with limited Navy participation.[31] According to the Navy, the W76-1 and other nuclear weapons modernization efforts are higher priorities than the W78/88-1 life-extension program and therefore Navy Strategic Systems Programs' participation in the warhead feasibility study was unfunded. Moreover, the Navy understands the Nuclear Weapons Council's requirement to enhance safety features, but has concerns that doing so would introduce uncertainty into the weapon's design.

The Air Force and NNSA Have Begun Examining Interoperable Warhead Designs

In September 2010, the Air Force and NNSA began a concept study to evaluate weapon design concepts that could be used in both the W78 and W88 life-extension programs. This effort focused on identifying options compatible with the Air Force's Mk12A aeroshell, which encases the W78 warhead, and the Navy's Mk5 aeroshell, which encases the W88 warhead.[32] Separately, in January 2012, NNSA sponsored an internal study by the nuclear weapons laboratories to develop additional

---

[30]For further discussion of the planning factors that U.S. Strategic Command considers in the targeting process, see GAO-12-786R.

[31]A concept study is performed by DOD, NNSA, or a project officers group under Phase 6.1 of the Phase 6.X process to determine whether a weapon in the stockpile requires refurbishment, and to investigate refurbishment concepts, such as interoperability. The study is expected to determine whether there exists sufficient interest in an idea for a nuclear weapon/component refurbishment to warrant further review. After completion of a Phase 6.1 concept study, either DOD, DOE, or the project officers group may submit a recommendation to the Nuclear Weapons Council to proceed with a feasibility study, under Phase 6.2.

[32]The Air Force did not consider the Mk21 in the study because at that time the Air Force was uncertain whether there were sufficient aeroshells configured for operational use.

concepts.[33] Together, the two studies identified a dozen designs that were potentially compatible with both Air Force and Navy ballistic missile systems.

Subsequently, the W78/88-1 Project Officers Group, the joint DOD-DOE body responsible for leading the feasibility study, has made progress in the study. By March 2013, the Nuclear Weapons Council had selected the Mk21 aeroshell, rather than the Mk12A aeroshell, for the Air Force version of the design.[34] Additionally, by July 2013 the Project Officers Group is expected to recommend using a single type of primary, which is a key component for the design.[35] Moreover, the Project Officers Group has agreed to limit the number of potential interoperable warhead design options that it would recommend to the Nuclear Weapons Council at the conclusion of the study.

The Navy Has Higher Nuclear Weapons Modernization Priorities and Has Concerns about Changing the Warhead Design

Although the Air Force and NNSA have made progress identifying and studying potential interoperable warhead designs, the Navy has had limited participation in the studies for the following reasons:

- The ongoing W76-1 life extension and W88 modernization are higher Navy priorities than the W78/88-1 life-extension program. Navy officials told us that the Navy's highest nuclear weapons modernization priority for NNSA is to complete the W76-1 life-extension program, which has been in production since 2008. Additionally, the Navy and NNSA are also modernizing the W88 warhead by developing a new arming, fuzing, and firing system,[36]

---

[33]NNSA requested that two design teams—one involving Lawrence Livermore National Laboratory and a second involving Los Alamos National Laboratory, with Sandia National Laboratories supporting both teams—evaluate alternatives for warhead designs to be deployed on multiple delivery systems. Each team was tasked to develop conceptual options for the W78 and W88 life-extension programs with each design compatible with both the Mk21 and Mk5 aeroshells.

[34]Because the Mk21 aeroshell is larger than the Mk12A, the feasibility study will have a broader range of options to consider for enhancing the safety and security of the design. The Navy version of the design would continue to be compatible with the Mk5 aeroshell, which is smaller than the Mk21.

[35]The nuclear primary component, together with the secondary component, makes up the weapon's nuclear explosive package.

[36]The arming, fuzing, and firing system is a nonnuclear component that controls the timing of the nuclear weapon's detonation.

which is to be installed on the warhead over a 5-year period beginning in fiscal year 2019. By contrast, the W78/88-1 life-extension program is a longer-term effort than these programs and, from the Navy's perspective, does not require the Navy's attention until the mid-2020s and after these more pressing needs are met. Therefore the Navy did not program funds for the warhead feasibility study in its fiscal year 2013 budget submission.

- The Navy has concerns about changing the warhead design. In its June 2012 approval of the start of the feasibility study, the Nuclear Weapons Council directed that the Project Officers Group investigate design options for an interoperable nuclear explosive package that included insensitive high explosive.[37] Navy officials noted that because the interoperable warhead is expected to involve a new design, it would require extensive flight testing and certification. Recognizing the Navy's concerns in November 2012, the Nuclear Weapons Council broadened the scope of the warhead feasibility study to also include options based on the existing W88 design, which does not use insensitive high explosive.

Because of its different priorities for modernization and concerns about introducing changes to the design of Navy warheads, the Navy has participated in the W78/88-1 life-extension program on a limited basis. The Navy was invited to take part in the Air Force's initial concept study in September 2010, but the Navy had neither the available staff nor the funding to fully contribute to the concept study. According to Navy Strategic Systems Programs officials, the Navy officials assigned to work on the W78/88-1 life-extension program did so only as a collateral duty without additional travel, overtime, or contractor support. Similarly, Navy and Air Force officials noted that although Navy officials had been named as coleaders of the W78/88-1 Project Officers Group and key subgroups for the warhead feasibility study, formal Navy participation in the study has been limited since the study began in June 2012. As a result, the Navy's contributions to the concept and feasibility studies have been limited to reviewing the military characteristics to ensure they were

---

[37]Insensitive high explosives are types of explosives used in some nuclear weapons because they are remarkably insensitive to shock, high temperatures, and impact when compared to conventional high explosives. As a result, the weapon is safer to handle and transport.

realistic for SLBM warheads,[38] according to Navy Strategic Systems Programs officials. The Air Force lead project officer added that the Navy's limited participation to date is delaying the Project Officers Group review of key requirements, engineering analyses, and design decisions until fiscal year 2014.

The Navy Has Identified Resources for the Warhead Feasibility Study, but Its Long-Term Support for the Program Remains Uncertain

The Navy has identified the required resources to support the study, but has not identified the long-term resource requirements needed to participate in later phases of the life-extension program, thereby making its commitment uncertain. In November 2012, the Navy offered to provide $43 million for the warhead feasibility study, but, according to Navy and Strategic Systems Programs officials, as of March 2013 the Navy had been unable to obligate any funds during fiscal year 2013 due to budget uncertainty and restrictions for operating under a continuing resolution.[39] However, the fiscal year 2014 budget submission included $14 million for fiscal year 2014 and $7 million for fiscal year 2015 for the Navy's participation in the study.

In the longer term, the Navy has not identified the resources needed to support the life-extension program, should the Nuclear Weapons Council approve of an interoperable design once the warhead feasibility study is completed. In preparing for the life-extension program's initial concept study, which the Air Force began in September 2010, the Office of the Secretary of Defense convened a Joint Requirements Working Group that identified several critical factors that should occur even before the start of the feasibility study.[40] Among these factors, the Joint Requirements Working Group recommended that the services and NNSA align their programs and identify and commit resources to the program early in the Phase 6.X process. The Air Force has established a program for the life-

---

[38]"Military characteristics" descr be a nuclear weapon's required size, shape, weight, and other physical attributes; performance characteristics, such as nuclear yields and heights-of-burst; safety and security standards, such as minimizing military personnel's radiation exposure; and other factors affecting nuclear weapons design.

[39]In May 2013, following the enactment of the Consolidated and Further Continuing Appropriations Act, 2013, Pub. L. No. 113-6 (2013), DOD sought to reprogram $3 million to support the Navy's participation in the warhead feasibility study.

[40]U.S. Strategic Command, *Joint Requirements Study for a Common Life Extension Program for the Mk12A/W78-1 and Mk5/W88-1*, Memorandum to the Assistant Secretary of Defense for Nuclear, Chemical, and Biological Defense Programs (Oct. 18, 2010).

extension effort, and in January 2013 the Air Force Nuclear Weapons Center estimated the costs for fiscal year 2016 through fiscal year 2018 to be about $5.5 million per year,[41] once the warhead feasibility study is complete. The Air Force lead project officer stated that these projected costs do not include additional funding needed for weapons system integration with the ICBM, adding that annual integration costs could grow to $20 million to $30 million by 2025, when the warhead is first being produced. By contrast, the Navy has not yet identified potential resource requirements beyond the feasibility study, and did not include such costs in its fiscal year 2014 budget submission.

The Navy's participation in the later phases of the W78/88-1 life-extension program remains uncertain because it has not identified the long-term resources that would be needed if the interoperable warhead is adopted. For example, DOD has not issued an implementing document for the 2010 Nuclear Posture Review that would require the Navy to identify such resources, even though the *Nuclear Posture Review Report* recommended studying options for developing an interoperable warhead during the W78 life-extension program, according to officials from the Office of the Secretary of Defense and the Navy. An official from the Under Secretary of Defense for Policy told us that the Navy would be directed to commit resources for the feasibility study through DOD's budgeting process, but the Navy has not been directed to identify the long-term costs associated with the effort.

Unless the Navy identifies the resources needed to support the later stages of the W78/88-1 life-extension program, should the Nuclear Weapons Council approve this step, then the Navy will be poorly positioned to perform more-detailed analysis, certification, and testing needed to validate the approved design, resulting in program delays. The costs of testing and certifying an interoperable warhead would likely be considerable, according to Navy officials, given the expectation that the warhead's design would be different than previously deployed warheads. During the phase of the 6.X process that comes after the feasibility and design definition and cost study phases, NNSA, in coordination with DOD, conducts tests, experiments, and analyses in order to validate the design options. At the end of this phase, the weapon's design needs to be

---

[41]In April 2013, the Air Force lead project officer stated that these costs were speculative until the fiscal year budget 2015 proposal was completed.

demonstrated to be feasible in terms of safety, use control, performance, reliability, and producibility. According to the NNSA federal program manager for SLBM warheads, significant differences exist between Air Force and Navy requirements, such that the Navy's participation during this phase would be needed in order to validate an interoperable warhead's design. Absent the Navy's identification of long-term funds, Navy officials acknowledged that the interoperable warhead's deployment on Navy systems could be delayed.

Guidelines for Refurbishing Warheads Do Not Require Program and Resource Alignment for Joint Warhead Studies

The guidance that governs warhead refurbishments, including life-extension programs, does not require the services to align their programs and resources in support of joint-service concept and feasibility studies conducted under the Phase 6.X process. This is because neither the Nuclear Weapons Council's *Procedural Guideline for the Phase 6.X Process*, nor DOD's implementing instruction 5030.55, *DOD Procedures for Joint DOD-DOE Nuclear Weapons Life-Cycle Activities*, have been updated to reflect the need for the Air Force and Navy to align their programs and resources early in the life-extension process, as the Joint Requirements Working Group recommended in 2010. For example, both the *Procedural Guideline* and DOD Instruction 5030.55 currently demonstrate coordination and conferral between DOD and DOE with respect to nuclear weapons activities. Additionally, DOD's instruction currently states that the military departments are to develop procedures for certain joint DOD-DOE activities. However, the *Procedural Guideline* and the instruction are unclear about the services' aligning their programs and resources with each other for supporting joint-service nuclear weapons concept and feasibility studies.

Both DOD and DOE have requirements to review and, as needed, update their respective guidance regularly. For example under the DOD Directives Program, DOD issuances—including directives, instructions, and other key publications—must be reviewed to determine whether they are necessary, current, and consistent with DOD policy, existing law, and statutory authority prior to the 5th year anniversary of their publication date.[42] The *Procedural Guideline for the Phase 6.X Process* was issued in 2000, and is now being updated, but the completion date of this task is uncertain. If the *Procedural Guideline for the Phase 6.X Process* and the

---

[42]*See* Department of Defense Instruction 5025.01, *DOD Directives Program*, para. 3.c (Sept. 26, 2012).

corresponding DOD instruction are not updated to reflect the need for the services to align their programs and identify resources to support joint-service nuclear weapons concept and feasibility studies, or unless other guidance is issued to this effect, then the individual services may not be prepared to fund future studies examining the feasibility of interoperable warheads.

Conclusions

DOD and NNSA are embarking on a long-term modernization of strategic delivery systems and the nuclear stockpile, which increasingly requires accurate information and close collaboration. The Nuclear Weapons Council has special roles and responsibilities related to synchronizing DOD and DOE efforts to modernize the nuclear weapons enterprise, and has adopted a long-term baseline plan for doing so. To this end, the council needs current and up-to-date cost estimates and other information from the Air Force and NNSA about a centerpiece of the 2010 *Nuclear Posture Review Report*—the long-term sustainment of the ICBM, together with interoperable warheads. Moreover, without considering which department will bear responsibility for the full cost of both the Minuteman III follow-on and the W78/88-1 warhead, both the Air Force and the council may be significantly underestimating the funds needed from DOD for the system's modernization. The conduct of the Minuteman III follow-on study may have implications for other nuclear weapon systems developments as the council revises its baseline plan. Therefore without Nuclear Weapons Council stakeholder involvement, the council's ability to synchronize its long-term plan will be limited.

At this time, the Navy has higher nuclear weapons modernization priorities and, coupled with long-standing concerns about introducing design changes to nuclear weapons, the Navy has been reluctant to fund its participation in the W78/88-1 feasibility study, contributing to the study's delay. However, unless the Navy identifies the long-term resources needed for the W78/88-1 life-extension program, it may be poorly positioned to undertake the more-detailed analyses needed to validate the interoperable warhead on Navy systems, resulting in further program delays and potentially costly modifications. Moreover, the Nuclear Weapons Council will lack the information that it needs to determine whether the interoperable warhead concept is an effective approach, both for the W78/88-1 life-extension program, and over the long term as a cornerstone for stockpile modernization. Further, unless the *Procedural Guideline for the Phase 6.X Process* and DOD Instruction 5030.55 are revised to ensure that the services align their programs and resources to jointly support future warhead concept and feasibility studies, or other such guidance is issued, the Nuclear Weapons Council's long-term vision for stockpile management, including the introduction of interoperable warheads, may be unattainable. Finally, unless the Navy identifies the long-term resource requirements for the warhead life-extension program, should the Nuclear Weapons Council approve an interoperable warhead design, then the Navy may be unable to fund the effort needed to test and certify the new design.

Recommendations for Executive Action

To assist DOD and DOE in synchronizing plans for modernizing the nuclear weapons enterprise and for assessing the feasibility of the interoperable warhead concept, we recommend the Secretary of Defense take the seven actions listed below, including three recommendations that are jointly addressed to the Secretary of Energy.

To enhance the Nuclear Weapons Council's ability to consider the development of the Minuteman III follow-on system and the W78/88-1 warhead as it synchronizes DOD and DOE modernization programs, we recommend the following four actions:

- The Secretaries of Defense and Energy direct the Secretary of the Air Force and NNSA Administrator to

    - prepare cost estimates that include the total system costs for Minuteman III follow-on system alternatives and the costs associated with the W78/88-1 warhead, and

    - provide periodic updates on the estimated total system cost to the Nuclear Weapons Council in conjunction with the Project Officers Group's semiannual program review.

- The Secretary of Defense direct the Secretary of the Air Force to update the draft study plan for the Minuteman III follow-on study by

    - including the Nuclear Weapons Council as a stakeholder to synchronize the Minuteman III follow-on study with the W78/88-1 life-extension program, and

    - providing periodic updates and a final report on the Minuteman III follow-on study to the Nuclear Weapons Council in conjunction with the Minuteman III follow-on study's periodic updates to its study advisory group.

To ensure that DOD and NNSA are able to consider the possibilities of potentially designing and developing an interoperable warhead as directed by the Nuclear Weapons Council during the W78/88-1 life-extension program, we recommend that the Secretary of Defense direct the Secretary of the Navy to identify the long-term resources needed to implement the W78/88-1 life-extension program once the warhead feasibility study is completed, should the Nuclear Weapons Council approve of an interoperable warhead design.

To ensure that the services are able to support the consideration of interoperable warhead concepts during future life-extension programs, we recommend the following two actions:

- the Secretaries of Defense and Energy direct the Nuclear Weapons Council to revise the *Procedural Guideline for the Phase 6.X Process* to require the services to align their programs and resources before beginning concept or feasibility studies jointly with another service; and

- the Secretary of Defense issue or revise existing guidance to require the services to align their programs and resources before beginning concept or feasibility studies jointly with another service.

Agency Comments and Our Evaluation

We provided DOD and DOE with copies of our draft classified report for their review and comment. In response, we received written comments from both departments, which are reprinted in appendixes II and III, respectively. DOD concurred with all seven recommendations, and DOE concurred with the three recommendations requiring joint action between the departments. DOD and DOE also provided technical comments, which we have incorporated as appropriate.

DOD and DOE concurred with our two recommendations that the Secretaries of Defense and Energy direct the Secretary of the Air Force and NNSA Administrator to (1) prepare cost estimates that include the total system costs for the Minuteman III follow-on system alternatives and the costs associated with the W78/88-1 warhead, and (2) provide periodic updates on the estimated total system cost to the Nuclear Weapons Council in conjunction with the W78/88-1 Project Officers Group's semiannual program review. In its response, DOD stated that the Air Force will outline the total life-cycle costs for the Minuteman III follow-on system as part of the Minuteman III follow-on study. DOD further stated that decisions about the Minuteman III follow-on and the W78/88-1 warhead will be informed by estimates of costs, schedule, and performance for the complete system, adding that total ownership costs would be agreed upon by DOD and NNSA. DOD also stated that it and NNSA would track progress via the Nuclear Weapons Council with semiannual updates from the Project Officers Group and through other acquisition reviews. In its response, DOE indicated that NNSA will prepare cost estimates that are suitable for discriminating among the options under consideration during the course of the warhead feasibility study, adding that a more-detailed cost estimate would be developed following the warhead feasibility study. DOE further indicated that although it could not speak for DOD, NNSA would work within the Nuclear Weapons Council and Project Officers Group structure—which includes the Air Force—to make parallel presentations of cost estimates for the Minuteman III follow-on system and the W78/88-1 warhead, as we recommended. Additionally, DOE indicated that NNSA and DOD could brief the council on estimated warhead costs and Minuteman III follow-on system costs, in conjunction with the Project Officers Group's semiannual program reviews. Our recommendations intend that the Nuclear Weapons Council receive total cost estimates periodically throughout the course of the Minuteman III follow-on study and the warhead feasibility study. If DOD's and DOE's proposed actions provide such periodic updates to the Nuclear Weapons Council and the presentations present a total system cost estimate in sufficient detail to affect the council's decision-making, then the intent of our recommendations will have been met.

DOD also concurred with our two recommendations that the Secretary of Defense direct the Secretary of the Air Force to update the draft study plan for the Minuteman III follow-on study by (1) including the Nuclear Weapons Council as a stakeholder to synchronize the Minuteman III follow-on study with the W78/88-1 life-extension program, and (2) providing periodic updates and a final report on the Minuteman III follow-on study to the Nuclear Weapons Council. In its response, DOD stated that the draft study plan includes the members of the Nuclear Weapons Council as stakeholders, adding that the council members are part of the study's senior advisory group, which would receive periodic updates from the Air Force study group. DOD stated further that it would provide additional briefings during the Minuteman III follow-on study to the council as requested. Our recommendation seeks to involve the Nuclear Weapons Council as a body in the Minuteman III follow-on study, so that the council is better informed about the course of the study, and can take actions to synchronize the development of a follow-on ICBM with other long-term nuclear weapons recapitalization plans. If DOD's actions provide the council with the information it needs for this purpose, then the intent of our recommendation will have been met.

DOD concurred with our recommendation that the Secretary of Defense direct the Secretary of the Navy to identify the long-term resources needed to implement the W78/88-1 life-extension program once the warhead feasibility study is completed, should the Nuclear Weapons Council approve of an interoperable warhead design. In its response, DOD stated that it supports Navy direction to identify the long-term resources needed to implement the W78/88-1 life-extension program once the warhead feasibility study is completed and the council approves a design. However, DOD did not provide information in its comments as to how it would implement this recommendation.

DOD and DOE concurred with our recommendation that the Secretaries of Defense and Energy direct the Nuclear Weapons Council to revise the *Procedural Guideline for the Phase 6.X Process* to require the services to align their programs and resources before beginning concept or feasibility studies jointly with another service. DOD stated that a revision to the Phase 6.X process is currently underway and will serve to align service programs and resources to support future warhead interoperability. In its response, DOE stated that NNSA will coordinate with DOD on the appropriate revisions. DOD also concurred with our recommendation that the Secretary of Defense issue or revise existing guidance to require the services to align their programs and resources before beginning concept or feasibility studies jointly with another service. In concurring with these recommendations, DOD stated further that the revision to the Phase 6.X process will acknowledge the requirement in existing departmental guidance that programs be fully resourced before major acquisition decisions. DOD added that the Nuclear Weapons Council and DOD's annual program review process will also provide forums to ensure technical, schedule, and resource alignment between the services and subsequently with NNSA.

We are sending copies of this report to the appropriate congressional committees and to the Secretary of Defense; Secretary of the Air Force; Secretary of the Navy; Chairman, Joint Chiefs of Staff; Commander, U.S. Strategic Command; Secretary of Energy; and Administrator, National Nuclear Security Administration (NNSA). This report is also available at no charge on the GAO website at http://www.gao.gov.

Should you or your staffs have any questions about this report, please contact John Pendleton at (202) 512-3489 or pendletonj@gao.gov. Contact points for our Offices of Congressional Relations and Public Affairs may be found on the last page of this report. GAO staff who made contributions to this report are listed in appendix IV.

John H. Pendleton
Director, Defense Capabilities and Management

List of Committees

The Honorable Carl Levin
Chairman
The Honorable James M. Inhofe
Ranking Member
Committee on Armed Services
United States Senate

The Honorable Dick Durbin
Chairman
The Honorable Thad Cochran
Ranking Member
Subcommittee on Defense
Committee on Appropriations
United States Senate

The Honorable Dianne Feinstein
Chairman
The Honorable Lamar Alexander
Ranking Member
Subcommittee on Energy and Water Development
Committee on Appropriations
United States Senate

The Honorable Howard P. McKeon
Chairman
The Honorable Adam Smith
Ranking Member
Committee on Armed Services
House of Representatives

The Honorable C.W. Bill Young
Chairman
The Honorable Pete Visclosky
Ranking Member
Subcommittee on Defense
Committee on Appropriations
House of Representatives

The Honorable Rodney Frelinghuysen
Chairman
The Honorable Marcy Kaptur
Ranking Member
Subcommittee on Energy and Water Development, and Related Agencies
Committee on Appropriations
House of Representatives

Appendix I: Scope and Methodology

For this review, we addressed the extent to which (1) the Department of Defense (DOD) has assessed the capability requirements, potential basing options, and costs for the follow-on to the Minuteman III intercontinental ballistic missile (ICBM); and (2) DOD and the National Nuclear Security Administration (NNSA) have explored the feasibility of incorporating an interoperable warhead concept into the long-term nuclear weapons stockpile plan. For our review of these two objectives, we obtained and analyzed DOD, NNSA, and Nuclear Weapons Council policies and guidance on the requirements development process and the planning and implementation of nuclear weapons delivery system modernization and stockpile life-extension programs. This documentation included: Chairman, Joint Chiefs of Staff Instruction 3170.01H, *Joint Capabilities Integration and Development System*, dated January 10, 2012; DOD Instruction 5030.55, *DOD Procedures for Joint DOD-DOE Nuclear Weapons Life-Cycle Activities*, dated June 25, 2001; and the Nuclear Weapons Council's *Procedural Guideline for the Phase 6.X Process*, dated April 2000. For criteria used in both objectives, we reviewed the April 2010 *Nuclear Posture Review Report*, particularly its analysis and recommendations for modernizing the Minuteman III ICBM and for studying the feasibility of developing interoperable warheads to be used on ICBMs and Navy submarine-launched ballistic missiles (SLBM).

To help us understand ICBM operational requirements, we traveled to Air Force Global Strike Command, Barksdale Air Force Base, Louisiana, and to U.S. Strategic Command, Offutt Air Force Base, Nebraska, to obtain briefings on ICBM operational requirements, readiness, maintenance, sustainment, and modernization, and to discuss these subjects with officials from each organization. We also reviewed Air Force instructions on ICBM readiness, operations, and maintenance. We obtained and reviewed key reports to Congress, including the May 2010, February 2011, and April 2012 reports to Congress from the Office of the Secretary of Defense that describe the administration's 10-year plan and cost estimates for modernizing nuclear weapons and their associated delivery systems. We also obtained and reviewed key Air Force documentation that provided additional details of the Air Force's plan to sustain the Minuteman III to 2030, and discussed this plan with Air Force Global Strike Command officials. We obtained and reviewed the 2011 Requirements and Planning Document, and a November 2012 update to that document that details DOD's requirements for deployed and nondeployed ICBM and SLBM warheads. We also obtained and reviewed the Nuclear Weapons Council's *Report on Stockpile Assessments for Fiscal Year 2011* in order to obtain a complete perspective on the safety, security, and effectiveness of the W78 and W88 warheads. We also obtained and reviewed NNSA's *Fiscal Year 2011 Stockpile Stewardship and Management Plan* and the *Technical Basis for Stockpile Transformation Planning–FY 2010* in order to put the proposal for developing interoperable warheads into context. We also interviewed DOD and NNSA officials responsible for developing and coordinating requirements for the follow-on to the Minuteman III ICBM and for the W78/88-1 life-extension program, and other officials from the Office of the Secretary of Defense, including from the office of the Deputy Assistant Secretary of Defense for Nuclear Matters and the Cost Assessment and Program Evaluation office; the Air Force, including Global Strike Command and Nuclear Weapons Center; the Navy, including Strategic Systems Programs; U.S. Strategic Command; and NNSA, including the NNSA manager for the W78/88-1 life-extension program and NNSA managers for the ICBM and SLBM weapons systems.

To determine the extent to which DOD has assessed the capability requirements and potential basing options for the follow-on to the Minuteman III ICBM, we analyzed the Air Force's initial capabilities document for the Minuteman III follow-on system, which identified minimum capability requirements for the future system and gaps in the current operating system. For an operational perspective, we met with officials from the Air Force Global Strike Command, Air Force Nuclear Weapons Center, Air Force A10, and U.S. Strategic Command to discuss such requirements and the Air Force's ability to maintain requirements at high levels of operational alert. To identify alternative basing options for the Minuteman III follow-on system, we reviewed previous basing reports such as the Land Based Strategic Deterrent analysis of alternatives, and Air Force documentation highlighting proposed alternative basing options prepared by the Air Force Nuclear Weapons Center and the Air Force Global Strike Command, which is leading the Minuteman III follow-on study. We discussed this documentation with officials from the Joint Staff, Air Force A10, Office of the Deputy Assistant Secretary of Defense for Nuclear Matters, Air Force Nuclear Weapons Center, and Air Force Global Strike Command.

After identifying capability requirements and alternative basing options, we reviewed the Air Force's draft plan for studying Minuteman III follow-on options, which was prepared by Air Force Global Strike Command. After reviewing the Air Force's draft study plan, we met with Air Force Global Strike Command and Air Force Nuclear Weapons Center officials to discuss, among other elements, how they planned to establish cost estimates for each of the alternative basing options, and the Air Force's plan for oversight for the planned study. Using our prior work for developing sound cost estimates found in *GAO Cost Estimating and Assessment Guide* as criteria,[1] we identified potential challenges to building comprehensive and credible cost estimates. Additionally, we reviewed statues and guidance related to the Nuclear Weapons Council, DOD, and Air Force processes for analyzing weapon system requirements, and used these documents as criteria to analyze the Nuclear Weapons Council's role in the Minuteman III follow-on study. We discussed and confirmed our approach with officials from the Office of the Secretary of Defense's Cost Assessment and Program Evaluation office, Office of the Deputy Assistant Secretary of Defense for Nuclear Matters, Office of the Deputy Assistant Secretary of Defense for Strategic and Tactical Systems, Air Force Global Strike Command, Air Force Nuclear Weapons Center, and Air Force A10.

To determine the extent to which DOD and NNSA have explored the feasibility of incorporating an interoperable warhead concept into the long-term nuclear weapons stockpile plan, we examined both the long-term plan and effort to date to implement the W78/88-1 life-extension program. We analyzed the Nuclear Weapons Council's preliminary baseline plan for the nuclear weapons stockpile for the next 25 years, including options that the council considered in adopting the baseline plan. We obtained and reviewed key briefings from U.S. Strategic Command, and interviewed officials from the Office of the Secretary of Defense, U.S. Strategic Command, NNSA, Air Force Nuclear Weapons Center, and Navy Strategic Systems Programs. We discussed possible uncertainties and risks about the baseline plan with officials from the Office of the Deputy Assistant Secretary of Defense for Nuclear Matters; U.S. Strategic Command; Air Force; and Navy. Turning to our analysis of the W78/88-1 life-extension program, we used criteria drawn from the 2010 *Nuclear Posture Review Report* and from the U.S. Strategic Command's 2010 *Joint Requirements Study for a Common Life Extension Program for the Mk12A/W78-1 and Mk5/W88-1*, and the *Procedural Guideline for the Phase 6.X Process*, to evaluate the extent to which the Air Force and Navy have aligned their programs and resources to support this effort. To perform this analysis, we

---

[1]GAO, *GAO Cost Estimating and Assessment Guide: Best Practices for Developing and Managing Capital Program Costs*, GAO-09-3SP (Washington, D.C.: March 2009).

- reviewed documentation for the W78/88-1 life-extension program, including memorandums from the Air Force, Navy, NNSA, and Nuclear Weapons Council;

- identified and reviewed key Air Force and NNSA briefings that identified potential design options for the W78/88-1 life-extension program;

- reviewed DOD, NNSA, and W78/88-1 Project Officer Group and subgroup charters, as well as Air Force, Navy, and NNSA budget documents;

- reviewed the Navy's perspective on stockpile modernization by interviewing senior officials from Navy Strategic Systems Programs, Navy N514, and NNSA's federal program manager for Navy warheads;

- interviewed the Air Force lead project officer and NNSA federal program manager for the W78/88-1 life-extension program, at Kirtland Air Force Base, New Mexico;

- interviewed NNSA officials involved in the management of the W78 and W88 warheads; and

- met with DOD officials, including officials from the Office of the Deputy Assistant Secretary of Defense for Nuclear Matters; Joint Staff J8; and U.S. Strategic Command.

We conducted this performance audit from June 2012 to June 2013 in accordance with generally accepted government auditing standards. Those standards require that we plan and perform the audit to obtain sufficient, appropriate evidence to provide a reasonable basis for our findings and conclusions based on our audit objectives. We believe that the evidence obtained provides a reasonable basis for our findings and conclusions based on our audit objectives.

Appendix II: Comments from the Department of Defense

THE ASSISTANT SECRETARY OF DEFENSE
3015 DEFENSE PENTAGON
WASHINGTON, DC 20301-3015

ACQUISITION

062113

Mr. John Pendleton
Director, Defense Capabilities and Management
U. S. Government Accountability Office
441 G Street, N.W.
Washington, DC 20548

Dear Mr. Pendleton:

This is the Department of Defense (DoD) response to the GAO Draft Report, GAO-13-463C, "ICBM MODERNIZATION: Approaches to Basing Options and Interoperable Warhead Designs Need Better Planning and Synchronization," dated April 18, 2013 (GAO Code 351739).

The DoD concurs with the draft report's four recommendations. I submitted separately a list of technical and factual errors for your consideration.

We appreciate the opportunity to comment on the draft report. My point of contact for this effort is Mr. Edward M. Hudak, Jr., Edward.Hudak@osd.mil or 703-614-1585.

Sincerely,

Katrina McFarland

Enclosure:
As stated

GAO DRAFT REPORT DATED APRIL 18, 2013
GA0-13-463C (GAO CODE 351739)

"ICBM MODERNIZATION: APPROACHES TO BASING OPTIONS AND
INTEROPERABLE WARHEAD DESIGNS NEED BETTER PLANNING AND
SYNCHRONIZATION"

DEPARTMENT OF DEFENSE COMMENTS
TO THE GAO RECOMMENDATIONS

RECOMMENDATION 1: To enhance the Nuclear Weapons Council's ability to
consider the development of the MMIII follow-on system and the W78/W88-1 warhead
as it synchronizes DoD and DOE modernization programs, we recommend the following
four actions:

- The Secretaries of Defense and Energy direct the SECAF and NNSA Administrator
  to:

  o Prepare cost estimates that include the total system costs for MMIII follow-on
    system alternatives and the costs associated with the W78/W88-1 warhead, and

  o Provide periodic updates on the estimated total system cost to the NWC in
    conjunction with the Project Officers Group's semiannual program review.

DOD RESPONSE: Concur. In the B61 Life Extension Program, DoD and NNSA,
through the Nuclear Weapons Council (NWC), have developed a strong working
relationship and processes that will be adapted to the ICBM Modernization program.
MM-III follow-on and W78/88-1 warhead decisions will be informed by estimates of
cost, schedule and performance for the complete system. Total ownership costs will be
agreed upon by the DoD and NNSA. The total life cycle cost for the MM-III follow-on
system will be outlined by the Air Force as part of the Ground Based Strategic Deterrent
(GBSD) Analysis of Alternatives (AoA). DoD's Cost Assessment and Program
Evaluation (CAPE) will perform an independent cost estimate of the program for the
upcoming Milestone A Defense Acquisition Board in FY 2015. W78/88-1 costs will be
determined by the joint DoD/NNSA Project Officer Group by June 2015. DoD's CAPE
will also prepare an independent cost estimate for the W78/88-1 program. DoD and
NNSA will track progress via the NWC with semi-annual updates from the Project
Officer Group and quarterly Defense Acquisition Execution System reports. Note that
the USD(AT&L) is both the DoD Milestone Decision Authority and the Chairman of the
NWC.

RECOMMENDATION 2: The SECDEF direct the SECAF to update the draft study
plan for the MMIII follow-on study by:

- Including the NWC as a stakeholder to synchronize the MMIII follow-on study with
  the W78/88-1 life-extension program; and

1

- Provide periodic updates and a final report on the MMIII follow-on study to the NWC in conjunction with the MMIII follow-on study's periodic updates to its study advisory group.

DOD RESPONSE: **Concur.** The draft study plan for GBSD includes the NWC members as stakeholders and they are an integral part of the GBSD AoA Senior Advisory Group. Coordination and synchronization will occur through periodic updates from the GBSD AoA to its Senior Advisory Group which includes AT&L, CAPE, Air Force, Navy, Policy USSTRATCOM, Joint Staff, Comptroller, and NNSA. Additional briefings to the NWC will be provided as requested during the AoA.

RECOMMENDATION 3: To ensure that DoD and NNSA are able to consider the possibilities of potentially designing and developing an interoperable warhead as directed by the NWC during the W78/88-1 life-extension program, we recommend that the SECDEF direct the Secretary of the Navy to identify the long-term resources needed to implement the W78/88-1 life-extension program once the warhead feasibility study is completed, should the NWC approve of an interoperable warhead design.

DOD RESPONSE: **Concur.** The Department supports Navy direction to identify the long-term resources needed to implement the W78/88-1 life-extension program once the warhead feasibility study is completed and the NWC approves a design.

RECOMMENDATION 4: To ensure that the services are able to support the consideration of interoperable warhead concepts during the future life-extension programs, we recommend the following action:

- The Secretaries of Defense and Energy direct the NWC to revise the Procedural Guidelines for the Phase 6.X Process to require the services to align their programs and resources before the beginning concept or feasibility studies jointly with another service; and

- The SECDEF issue or revise existing guidance to require the services to align their programs and resources before beginning concept or feasibility studies jointly with another service.

DOD RESPONSE: **Concur.** A revision to the Phase 6.X process is underway and will serve to align Service programs and resources to support future warhead interoperability. The revision will acknowledge the DoD 5000.02 requirement that programs be fully resourced before major acquisition decisions. The NWC and DoD's annual Program Review process will also provide forums to ensure technical, schedule and resource alignment between Services and subsequent alignment with NNSA.

2

Appendix III: Comments from the Department of Energy

Department of Energy
National Nuclear Security Administration
Washington, DC 20585

May 24, 2013

Mr. John H. Pendleton
Director
Defense Capabilities and Management
Government Accountability Office
Washington, DC 20458

Dear Mr. Pendleton,

The National Nuclear Security Administration (NNSA) appreciates the opportunity to review the Government Accountability Office's (GAO) draft report, "ICBM Modernization: Approaches to Basing Options and Interoperable Warhead Designs Need Better Planning and Synchronization," GAO-13-463C. GAO conducted this audit in response to a congressional mandate in Public Law 11-81, Section 1047, Comptroller General Report on Nuclear Weapons Capabilities and Force Structure Requirements. GAO was asked to assess the extent to which the Department of Defense (DOD) has: (1) determined the force structure and capability requirements for Intercontinental Ballistic Missiles (ICBMs), (2) synchronized those requirements with plans to extend the service life of ICBM warheads, and (3) evaluated long-term ICBM alert posture requirements and basing options.

The GAO provided seven recommendations to the Secretary of Defense, three of which require joint action by the NNSA to assist in synchronization of plans for modernizing the nuclear weapons enterprise and for assessing feasibility of the interoperable warhead concept. NNSA concurs with the recommendations identified in the report. The enclosure to this letter provides our specific responses to each of the report recommendations. We have also enclosed general and technical comments for your consideration to improve the factual accuracy and clarity of the report.

If you have any questions concerning this response, please contact Dean Childs, Director, Office of Audit Coordination and Internal Affairs, at (301) 903-1341.

Sincerely,

Cynthia A. Lersten
Associate Administrator
for Management and Budget

Enclosure

Printed with soy ink on recycled paper

**National Nuclear Security Administration Response to
the Government Accountability Office Draft Report Titled
*"ICBM Modernization: Approaches to Basing Options and Interoperable
Warhead Designs Need Better Planning and Synchronization"* (GAO-13-463C)**

**The Government Accountability Office (GAO) recommended the Secretary of Energy
direct the National Nuclear Security Administration (NNSA) to:**

<u>Recommendation 1</u>: Prepare cost estimates that include the total system costs for the
Minuteman III follow-on system alternatives and the costs associated with the W78/88-1
warhead.

Management Response: Concur

In 2012, NNSA completed the *Phase 6.1 (Concept Assessment)* of the W78/88-1 Life Extension
Study and is currently in *Phase 6.2 (Feasibility Study and Option Down-Select)* of the Phase 6.X
Process as directed by and coordinated with the Nuclear Weapons Council (NWC). Given the
maturity of the warhead design concept options being investigated and developed, NNSA will
prepare cost estimates suitable for discriminating the alternatives considered. NNSA cost
estimates for design options will have the resolution to usefully compare alternatives. As
required by the Phase 6.X Process, a more detailed cost estimate will be developed during *Phase
6.2A (Design Definition and Cost Study)*, at which time the NNSA will develop and publish a
Weapon Design and Cost Report (WDCR) for the refurbishment of the W78/88-1 warhead. The
W78/88-1 LEP Project Officers Group (POG) will present the NNSA WDCR cost estimate to the
NWC shortly thereafter and could include the DOD cost estimates for the objective Minuteman
III follow-on system alternatives. The NNSA will support the POG to provide a
recommendation to the NWC on whether or not to proceed to *Phase 6.3 (Development
Engineering)* for the W78/88-1 LEP and could synchronize with Minuteman III follow-on
alternatives.

NNSA cannot speak for DOD, but NNSA will work within the NWC and POG organizational
structure to recommend the parallel presentations of comparable cost estimates explicitly
recommended here by GAO.

<u>Recommendation 2</u>: Provide periodic updates on the estimated total system cost to the NWC in
conjunction with the POG's semiannual program review.

Management Response: Concur

Upon NWC's *Phase 6.3* authorization, the NNSA will develop and submit an initial Selected
Acquisition Report (SAR) to Congress. NNSA will base the initial SAR on the WDCR. The
SAR will contain development and production costs of the warhead and is required to be updated
quarterly through the life of the acquisition program. NNSA will continue to prepare cost
estimates for the W78/88-1 warhead consistent with congressional and NWC requirements.
NNSA could brief the NWC on estimated W78/88-1 warhead costs once the SAR is developed.
If DOD develops and updates a DOD Minuteman III Follow-On SAR, "periodic updates on the

estimated total system cost" could be available for the NWC in conjunction with the POG semiannual program review.

The GAO recommended the Secretary of Defense and the Secretary of Energy direct the Nuclear Weapons Council to:

<u>Recommendation 3</u>: Revise the *Procedural Guideline for the Phase 6.X Process* to require the services to align their programs and resources before beginning concept or feasibility studies jointly with another service.

Management Response: Concur

NNSA will coordinate with the DOD on the appropriate revisions to the *Procedural Guideline for the Phase 6.X Process.*

Appendix IV: GAO Contact and Staff Acknowledgments

GAO Contact	John H. Pendleton, (202) 512-3489 or pendletonj@gao.gov
Staff Acknowledgments	In addition to the contact named above, key contributors to this report included Penney Harwell Caramia, Assistant Director; David M. Adams; Colin Chambers; Grace Coleman; Julie Corwin; Robert Scott Fletcher; Jason Lee; Kevin L. O'Neill; Michael Shaughnessy; and Amie Steele.

(351848)

GAO's Mission	The Government Accountability Office, the audit, evaluation, and investigative arm of Congress, exists to support Congress in meeting its constitutional responsibilities and to help improve the performance and accountability of the federal government for the American people. GAO examines the use of public funds; evaluates federal programs and policies; and provides analyses, recommendations, and other assistance to help Congress make informed oversight, policy, and funding decisions. GAO's commitment to good government is reflected in its core values of accountability, integrity, and reliability.
Obtaining Copies of GAO Reports and Testimony	The fastest and easiest way to obtain copies of GAO documents at no cost is through GAO's website (http://www.gao.gov). Each weekday afternoon, GAO posts on its website newly released reports, testimony, and correspondence. To have GAO e-mail you a list of newly posted products, go to http://www.gao.gov and select "E-mail Updates."
Order by Phone	The price of each GAO publication reflects GAO's actual cost of production and distribution and depends on the number of pages in the publication and whether the publication is printed in color or black and white. Pricing and ordering information is posted on GAO's website, http://www.gao.gov/ordering.htm. Place orders by calling (202) 512-6000, toll free (866) 801-7077, or TDD (202) 512-2537. Orders may be paid for using American Express, Discover Card, MasterCard, Visa, check, or money order. Call for additional information.
Connect with GAO	Connect with GAO on Facebook, Flickr, Twitter, and YouTube. Subscribe to our RSS Feeds or E-mail Updates. Listen to our Podcasts. Visit GAO on the web at www.gao.gov.
To Report Fraud, Waste, and Abuse in Federal Programs	Contact: Website: http://www.gao.gov/fraudnet/fraudnet.htm E-mail: fraudnet@gao.gov Automated answering system: (800) 424-5454 or (202) 512-7470
Congressional Relations	Katherine Siggerud, Managing Director, siggerudk@gao.gov, (202) 512-4400, U.S. Government Accountability Office, 441 G Street NW, Room 7125, Washington, DC 20548
Public Affairs	Chuck Young, Managing Director, youngc1@gao.gov, (202) 512-4800 U.S. Government Accountability Office, 441 G Street NW, Room 7149 Washington, DC 20548

Please Print on Recycled Paper.